to Write Hiragana and Katakana Characters

The strokes of hiragana and katakana are always written from left to right and from top to bottom. Each stroke will have one of the following types of ending: とめ **tome** (stop), はね **hane** (jump) or はらい **harai** (sweep). A stop is when the stroke comes to a stop before you move your pen from the paper. A jump is a small flourish made by removing the pen from the paper as you move to the next stroke. A sweep is when the pen is slowly removed from the end of the stroke in a sweeping motion. In the letter **ke** shown on the right, stroke 1 is a jump, stroke 2 is a stop and stroke 3 is a sweep.

Instructions for Writing the Hiragana Characters

shi し	sa さ	ko こ	ke け	ku く	ki き	ka か	o お	e え	u う	i い	a あ

ne ね	nu ぬ	ni に	na な	to と	te て	tsu つ	chi ち	ta た	so そ	se せ	su す

やもめむみまほへふひはの

ゆよらりるれろわをん

Instructions for Writing the Katakana Characters

shi シ	sa サ	ko コ	ke ケ	ku ク	ki キ	ka カ	o オ	e エ	u ウ	i イ	a ア

ne ネ	nu ヌ	ni ニ	na ナ	to ト	te テ	tsu ツ	chi チ	ta タ	so ソ	se セ	su ス

ya	mo	me	mu	mi	ma	ho	he	fu	hi	ha	no
ヤ	モ	メ	ム	ミ	マ	ホ	ヘ	フ	ヒ	ハ	ノ

		n	(w)o	wa	ro	re	ru	ri	ra	yo	yu
		ン	ヲ	ワ	ロ	レ	ル	リ	ラ	ヨ	ユ

How to Write Kanji Characters

To write kanji legibly, it is important to know how each stroke is drawn. Here are some principles and tendencies for stroke endings, stroke directions and stroke orders, followed by writing practice exercises for 35 basic characters.

Stroke Order

You should remember how the strokes in each character are ordered in order to write a character neatly with the appropriate shape. Most kanji characters are written following the general principles of stroke order:

1. From top to bottom.

三 (three) 一 二 三

2. From left to right.

川 (river) ノ 丿丨 川

3. Horizontal strokes usually precede vertical strokes when crossing, although there are some exceptions such as 王 and 田.

十 (ten) 一 十

4. A central line usually precedes the strokes placed on its right and left.

小 (small) 亅 小 小

5. An outer frame must be written first before finishing the inside except for the bottom line. The bottom line of an outer frame must be completed at the very end.

国 (country) 丨 冂 国 国

6. A right-to-left diagonal stroke precedes a left-to-right diagonal stroke.

人 (person) ノ 人

7. A vertical line piercing through the center of a character is written last.

車 (vehicle) 一 百 亘 車

8. A horizontal line piercing the center of the character is written last.

子 (child)

Stroke Endings

Each stroke ends in とめ **tome** (stop), はね **hane** (jump) or はらい **harai** (sweep). (Note that some diagonal lines end in stop-sweep.) For example, a vertical straight line can end in stop, jump, or sweep, as shown below:

とめ **tome** (stop)	はね **hane** (jump)	はらい **harai** (sweep)

Stroke Directions

A stroke can be vertical, horizontal, diagonal, angled, or curved, or can be just a short abbreviated line. *Vertical lines* always go from top to bottom, and *horizontal lines* always go from left to right.

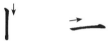

Diagonal lines can go either downward or upward. For example:

If a stroke forms a corner, a sharp angle, or a curve, it goes from left to right and then goes down, or goes down and then left to right. For example:

corner

sharp angle

curve

Some strokes have a combination of a sharp angle and a curve. For example:

Some strokes are extremely short and are called てん **ten**. They may be vertical or slightly diagonal:

六	五	四	三	二	一
roku/mu- **six**	go/itsu- **five**	shi/yo- **four**	san/mi- **three**	ni/futa- **two**	ichi/hito- **one**

6

千	百	十	九	八	七
sen/chi **1,000**	hyaku **100**	jū/tō- **ten**	kyū/kokono- **nine**	hachi/ya- **eight**	shichi/nana- **seven**

水		火		月		日		円		万	
sui/mizu **water**		hi/ho/ka **fire**		tsuki/gatsu **moon/month**		nichi/hi **sun/day**		en/maru- **yen/circle**		man/ban **10,000**	

時	年	週	土	金	木
ji/toki **time**	nen/toshi **year**	shū **week**	do/to/tsuchi **earth**	kin/kane **gold**	moku/ki **wood/tree**

9

今	後	前	午	分	間
kon/ima **now**	go/ushi- **after**	zen/mae **before**	go/uma **noon**	bun//fun//wa- **minute**	kan/aida **between**

10

男	女	山	川	何	半
dan/otoko **man**	jo/onna **woman**	san/yama **mountain**	sen/kawa **river**	ka/nani/nan **what**	han/naka- **half**

男
女
山
川
何
半

外	中	下	上	友	子
gai/soto **outside**	chū/naka **middle**	ge/ka/shita **below**	jō/shō/ue **above**	to yū/tomo **friend**	shi/ko **child**

🎧 The 46 Basic Hiragana Characters

The chart below shows the 46 basic characters in the hiragana alphabet with their pronunciation. Hiragana is generally used for grammatical endings and words that don't have kanji.

お o	え e	う u	い i	あ a
こ ko	け ke	く ku	き ki	か ka
そ so	せ se	す su	し shi	さ sa
と to	て te	つ tsu	ち chi	た ta
の no	ね ne	ぬ nu	に ni	な na
ほ ho	へ he (e)	ふ fu	ひ hi	は ha (wa)
も mo	め me	む mu	み mi	ま ma
よ yo		ゆ yu		や ya
ろ ro	れ re	る ru	り ri	ら ra
を w(o)				わ wa
				ん n

🎧 The 61 Additional Hiragana Characters

Adding two small lines to a hiragana syllable makes the sound hard. **Ka** becomes **ga**, **sa** becomes **za**, etc. Adding a small circle to the syllables starting with **h** makes a **p** sound. In the lower two tables the **i**-column syllable combines with **ya**, **yu** or **yo** to make the sounds **kya**, **kyu**, **kyo**, etc.

ご go	げ ge	ぐ gu	ぎ gi	が ga
ぞ zo	ぜ ze	ず zu	じ ji	ざ za
ど do	で de	づ zu	ぢ ji	だ da
ぼ bo	べ be	ぶ bu	び bi	ば ba
ぽ po	ぺ pe	ぷ pu	ぴ pi	ぱ pa

じょ jo	じゅ ju	じゃ ja
ぢょ jo	ぢゅ ju	ぢゃ ja
みょ myo	みゅ myu	みゃ mya
りょ ryo	りゅ ryu	りゃ rya
びょ byo	びゅ byu	びゃ bya
ぴょ pyo	ぴゅ pyu	ぴゃ pya

きょ kyo	きゅ kyu	きゃ kya
しょ sho	しゅ shu	しゃ sha
ちょ cho	ちゅ chu	ちゃ cha
にょ nyo	にゅ nyu	にゃ nya
ひょ hyo	ひゅ hyu	ひゃ hya
ぎょ gyo	ぎゅ gyu	ぎゃ gya

The 46 Basic Katakana Characters

The chart below shows the 46 basic characters in the katakana alphabet with their pronunciation. Katakana is used for writing foreign loan words, for emphasis and for onomatopoeia.

オ o	エ e	ウ u	イ i	ア a
コ ko	ケ ke	ク ku	キ ki	カ ka
ソ so	セ se	ス su	シ shi	サ sa
ト to	テ te	ツ tsu	チ chi	タ ta
ノ no	ネ ne	ヌ nu	ニ ni	ナ na
ホ ho	ヘ h(e)	フ fu	ヒ hi	ハ ha/wa
モ mo	メ me	ム mu	ミ mi	マ ma
ヨ yo		ユ yu		ヤ ya
ロ ro	レ re	ル ru	リ ri	ラ ra
ヲ w(o)				ワ wa
				ン n

The 50 Additional Katakana Characters

Adding two small lines to a katakana syllable makes the sound hard. **Ka** becomes **ga**, **sa** becomes **za**, etc. Adding a small circle to the syllables starting with **h** makes a **p** sound. In the lower two tables the **i**-column syllable combines with **ya**, **yu** or **yo** to make the sounds **kya**, **kyu**, **kyo**, etc.

ゴ **go**	ゲ **ge**	グ **gu**	ギ **gi**	ガ **ga**
ゾ **zo**	ゼ **ze**	ズ **zu**	ジ **ji**	ザ **za**
ド **do**	デ **de**			ダ **da**
ボ **bo**	ベ **be**	ブ **bu**	ビ **bi**	バ **ba**
ポ **po**	ペ **pe**	プ **pu**	ピ **pi**	パ **pa**

ギョ **gyo**	ギュ **gyu**	ギャ **gya**
ジョ **jo**	ジュ **ju**	ジャ **ja**
ミョ **myo**	ミュ **myu**	ミャ **mya**
リョ **ryo**	リュ **ryu**	リャ **rya**

キョ **kyo**	キュ **kyu**	キャ **kya**
ショ **sho**	シュ **shu**	シャ **sha**
チョ **cho**	チュ **chu**	チャ **cha**
ニョ **nyo**	ニュ **nyu**	ニャ **nya**
ヒョ **hyo**	ヒュ **hyu**	ヒャ **hya**

105 Common Kanji Characters

These kanji are often encountered at level N5 of the JLPT test. Beneath each kanji is the English meaning, the *on-yomi* in capitals (the reading generally used in words made up of more than one kanji character), and the *kun-yomi* in bold (the reading generally used for words with one kanji).

七 seven SHICHI **nana-**	六 six ROKU **mu-**	五 five GO **itsu-**	四 four SHI **yo-**	三 three SAN **mi-**	二 two NI **futa-**	一 one ICHI **hito-**
円 yen/circle EN **maru-**	万 10,000 MAN/BAN **no kun reading**	千 1,000 SEN **chi**	百 100 HYAKU **no kun reading**	十 ten JŪ **tō-**	九 nine KYŪ **kokono-**	八 eight HACHI **ya-**
土 earth DO/TO **tsuchi**	金 gold KIN **kane**	木 wood/tree MOKU **ki**	水 water SUI **mizu**	火 fire HI/HO **ka**	月 moon/month TSUKI **gatsu/getsu**	日 sun/day NICHI/JITSU **hi/ka**
前 before ZEN **mae**	午 noon GO **uma-**	分 minute BUN/FUN **wa-**	間 between KAN/KEN **aida/ma**	時 time JI **toki**	年 year NEN **toshi**	週 week SHŪ **no kun reading**
人 person JIN/NIN **hito**	何 what KA **nani/nan**	毎 every MAI **goto**	半 half HAN **naka-**	先 ahead SEN **saki**	今 now KON/KIN **ima**	後 after GO **ushi-**
本 book HON **moto**	友 friend YŪ **tomo**	父 father FU **chichi**	母 mother BO **haha**	子 child SHI/SU **ko**	男 man DAN **otoko**	女 woman JO **onna**
雨 rain U **ame**	生 life SEI/SHŌ **i-/u-**	気 spirit KI/KE **iki**	天 heaven TEN **ama-**	空 sky KŪ **sora**	山 mountain SAN **yama**	川 river SEN **kawa**

耳 ear JI mimi	目 eye MOKU me	口 mouth KŌ/KU kuchi	語 word GO kata-	魚 fish GYO uo/sakana	車 car SHA kuruma	電 electricity DEN no kun reading
社 company SHA yashiro	道 road DŌ michi	駅 station EKI no kun reading	店 shop TEN mise	名 name MEI na	足 leg/foot SOKU ashi	手 hand SHU te
中 middle CHŪ naka	下 below GE/KA shita	上 above JŌ/SHŌ ue	外 outside GAI soto	校 school KO/KYO no kun reading	学 study GAKU mana-	国 country KOKU kuni
聞 hear/ask BUN/MON ki(ku)	東 east TŌ higashi	西 west SEI/SAI nishi	南 south NAN minami	北 north HOKU kita	左 left SA hidari	右 right U/YŪ migi
行 go KŌ i(ku)	買 buy BAI ka(u)	言 say GEN i(u)	話 speak WA hana(su)	書 write SHO ka(ku)	読 read DOKU yo(mu)	見 see KEN mi(ru)
立 stand RITSU ta(tsu)	食 eat SHOKU tabe(ru)	飲 drink IN no(mu)	休 rest/day off KYŪ yasu(mu)	出 go out SHUTSU de(ru)	入 go in NYŪ i(ru)	来 come RAI ku(ru)
高 high/expensive KŌ taka-	安 low/cheap AN yasu-	多 many TA ō-	少 few/little SHŌ suku(nai)/suko(shi)	小 small SHŌ chī-/ko-	大 big DAI/TAI ō-	会 meet KAI a(u)
引 pull IN hi-	英 England EI hanabusa	好 like KŌ kono-/su-	思 think SHI omo-	世 world SEI yo	新 new SHIN atara-/ara-	古 old KO furu-

🎧 100 Common Kanji Vocabulary Words

These vocabulary words are ones that commonly appear in the JLPT N5 test. They include compounds that use the kanji introduced on pages 124–125 as well as common verbs and adjectives that use kanji. Each vocabulary word is presented in three columns, with its kanji reading, its kana reading and its English translation.

#	Kanji	Kana	English	#	Kanji	Kana	English
26	今週	こんしゅう	this week	1	一人	ひとり	one person
27	来月	らいげつ	next month	2	二人	ふたり	two people
28	先月	せんげつ	last month	3	三人	さんにん	three people
29	時間	じかん	time	4	四月	しがつ	April
30	十分	じゅっぷん	10 minutes	5	五月	ごがつ	May
31	午前	ごぜん	a.m.	6	六月	ろくがつ	June
32	午後	ごご	p.m.	7	七日	なのか	7th (date)
33	日中	にっちゅう	during the day	8	八日	ようか	8th (date)
34	上着	うわぎ	overcoat, jacket	9	九日	ここのか	9th (date)
35	靴下	くつした	socks	10	十日	とうか	10th (date)
36	名前	なまえ	name	11	千円	せんえん	1,000 yen
37	外国人	がいこくじん	foreigner	12	百万円	ひゃくまんえん	1 million yen
38	外国語	がいこくご	foreign language	13	万年筆	まんねんひつ	fountain pen
39	日本語	にほんご	Japanese language	14	日曜日	にちようび	Sunday
40	英語	えいご	English language	15	月曜日	げつようび	Monday
41	女の子	おんなのこ	girl	16	火曜日	かようび	Tuesday
42	男の子	おとこのこ	boy	17	水曜日	すいようび	Wednesday
43	子供	こども	child	18	木曜日	もくようび	Thursday
44	花火	はなび	fireworks	19	金曜日	きんようび	Friday
45	生徒	せいと	student	20	土曜日	どようび	Saturday
46	天気	てんき	weather	21	毎日	まいにち	every day
47	電気	でんき	electricity	22	今日	きょう	today
48	元気	げんき	well, fine, healthy	23	明日	あした	tomorrow
49	手紙	てがみ	letter	24	昨日	きのう	yesterday
50	喫茶店	きっさてん	coffee shop	25	何日	なんにち	what day?

76	食べ物	たべもの	food		51	駅前	えきまえ	in front of the station
77	飲む	のむ	to drink		52	道具	どうぐ	tool
78	飲み物	のみもの	drink(s)		53	会社	かいしゃ	company
79	買う	かう	to buy		54	社長	しゃちょう	company president
80	買い物	かいもの	shopping		55	大学	だいがく	university
81	休む	やすむ	to rest; take a holiday		56	学校	がっこう	school
82	立つ	たつ	to stand		57	東京	とうきょう	Tokyo
83	大きい	おおきい	big		58	見る	みる	to look; see
84	大変	たいへん	dreadful, awful		59	見せる	みせる	to show
85	小さい	ちいさい	small		60	聞く	きく	to ask; listen
86	高い	たかい	high; expensive		61	新聞	しんぶん	newspaper
87	安い	やすい	low; cheap		62	書く	かく	to write
88	多い	おおい	many		63	辞書	じしょ	dictionary
89	多分	たぶん	perhaps		64	読む	よむ	to read
90	少ない	すくない	few		65	言う	いう	to say
91	少し	すこし	a little		66	話す	はなす	to speak
92	古い	ふるい	old		67	電話	でんわ	telephone
93	新しい	あたらしい	new		68	行く	いく	to go
94	長い	ながい	long		69	銀行	ぎんこう	bank
95	部長	ぶちょう	office manager		70	来る	くる	to come
96	短い	みじかい	short		71	出かける	でかける	to go out
97	黒い	くろい	black (adj.)		72	出口	でぐち	exit
98	白い	しろい	white (adj.)		73	入る	はいる	to go in
99	面白い	おもしろい	interesting		74	入口	いりぐち	entrance
100	円い	まるい	round		75	食べる	たべる	to eat

Plain Verb Forms in Japanese

There are 4 groups of Japanese verbs: -ru verbs, -u verbs, irregular verbs and special polite verbs, each with a root and a stem. The root is the unchanged core of a verb. The stem is the part of the verb before -masu. For -ru verbs, the root and stem are the same, ending either in /e/ or /i/. The root of -u verbs ends in one of 9 consonants (b, k, g, m, n, r, t, s, w), and the stem is the root plus /i/ added at the end. Past Affirmative forms vary according to the consonant. The sound /w/ drops before a vowel, except /a/. Thus /kawu/ becomes /kau/.

Negative			Affirmative			
Te Form	Past	Non-Past	Te Form	Past	Non-Past	
Verb + nakute	*Verb* + nakatta	*Verb* + nai	*Verb* + te	*Verb* + ta	*Verb* + ru	*ru* verbs
wakaranakute	wakaranakatta	wakaranai	wakatte	wakatta	waka**ru**	*u* verbs
matanakute	matanakatta	matanai	matte	matta	ma**tsu**	
kawanakute	kawanakatta	kawanai	katte	katta	ka(**w**)u	The largest
asobanakute	asobanakatta	asobanai	asonde	asonda	aso**bu**	group
nomanakute	nomanakatta	nomanai	nonde	nonda	no**mu**	
shinanakute	shinanakatta	shinanai	shinde	shinda	shi**nu**	
kikanakute	kikanakatta	kikanai	kiite	kiita	ki**ku**	
oyoganakute	oyoganakatta	oyoganai	oyoide	oyoida	oyo**gu**	
hanasanakute	hanasanakatta	hanasanai	hanashite	hanashita	hana**su**	
konakute	konakatta	konai	kite	kita	kuru	Four Irregular
shinakute	shinakatta	shinai	shite	shita	suru	Verbs
nakute	nakatta	nai	atte	atta	aru	
ikanakute	ikanakatta	ikanai	itte	itta	iku	
irassharanakute	irassharanakatta	irassharanai	irasshatte	irasshatta	irassharu	Five Special
ossharanakute	ossharanakatta	ossharanai	osshatte	osshatta	ossharu	Polite Verbs
nasaranakute	nasaranakatta	nasaranai	nasatte	nasatta	nasaru	
kudasaranakute	kudasaranakatta	kudasaranai	kudasatte	kudasatta	kudasaru	
gozaranakute	gozaranakatta	gozaranai	gozatte	gozatta	gozaru	

ru verbs: Non-Past Affirmative: Verb Stem + /ru/
Past Affirmative: Verb Stem + /ta/
Te Form: Verb Stem + /te/
Non-Past Negative: Verb Stem + /nai/
Past Negative: Verb Stem + /nakatta/
Negative Te Form: Verb Stem + /nakute/

u verbs: Non-Past Affirmative: Change the Stem final /i/ to /u/
Past Affirmative: Verb Root + /ta/
Root endings /r/, /t/, or /w/ + /ta/ become /tta/
Root endings /b/, /m/, or /n/ +/ta/ become /nda/
Root ending /k/ + /ta/ becomes /ita/
Root ending /g/ + /ta/ becomes /ida/
Root ending /s/ + /ta/ becomes /shita/
Te Form: Change /ta/ in the Past form to /te/
Non-Past Negative: Verb Root + /anai/
Past Negative: Verb Root + /anakatta/
Negative Te Form: Change /nakatta/ in the past negative form to /nakute/

"Books to Span the East and West"

Tuttle Publishing was founded in 1832 in the small New England town of Rutland, Vermont [USA]. C
core values remain as strong today as they were then—to publish best-in-class books which bring people
together one page at a time. In 1948, we established a publishing office in Japan—and Tuttle is now a
leader in publishing English-language books about the arts, languages and cultures of Asia. The world has
become a much smaller place today and Asia's economic and cultural influence has grown. Yet the need for
meaningful dialogue and information about this diverse region has never been greater. Over the past seven
decades, Tuttle has published thousands of books on subjects ranging from martial arts and paper crafts to
language learning and literature—and our talented authors, illustrators, designers and photographers have
won many prestigious awards. We welcome you to explore the wealth of information available on Asia at
www.tuttlepublishing.com.

Published by Tuttle Publishing, an imprint of
Periplus Editions (HK) Ltd.

www.tuttlepublishing.com

Copyright © 2022 by Periplus Editions (HK) Ltd
Page 5 courtesy Eriko Sato
Page 127 courtesy Emiko Konomi

Library of Congress Cataloging-in-Publication Data

ISBN 978-4-8053-1712-9

Distributed by

North America, Latin America & Europe
Tuttle Publishing
364 Innovation Drive
North Clarendon, VT 05759-9436 U.S.A.
Tel: 1 (802) 773-8930
Fax: 1 (802) 773-6993
info@tuttlepublishing.com
www.tuttlepublishing.com

Japan
Tuttle Publishing
Yaekari Building 3rd Floor
5-4-12 Osaki
Shinagawa-ku
Tokyo 141-0032
Tel: (81) 3 5437-0171
Fax: (81) 3 5437-0755
sales@tuttle.co.jp
www.tuttle.co.jp

Asia Pacific
Berkeley Books Pte. Ltd.
3 Kallang Sector #04-01
Singapore 349278
Tel: (65) 6741 2178
Fax: (65) 6741 2179
inquiries@periplus.com.sg
www.tuttlepublishing.com

26 25 24 23 22
2207TP   10 9 8 7 6 5 4 3 2 1

Printed in Singapore

TUTTLE PUBLISHING₀ is a registered trademark of Tuttle
Publishing, a division of Periplus Editions (HK) Ltd.